THE ELEMENTS

Phosphorus

Richard Beatty

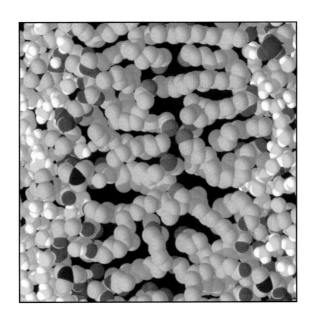

BENCHMARK BOOKS

MARSHALL CAVENDISH
NEW YORK

Benchmark Books
Marshall Cavendish Corporation
99 White Plains Road
Tarrytown, New York 10591

Library of Congress Cataloging-in-Publication Data
Beatty, Richard.
Phosphorus / Richard Beatty.
p.   cm. — (The elements)
Includes index.
Summary: Explores the history of the nonmetallic element phosphorus
and explains its chemistry, its reactions with other substances, its uses, and
its importance in our lives.
ISBN 0-7614-0946-7 (lib. bdg.)
1. Phosphorus—Juvenile literature. [1. Phosphorus.] I. Title.
II. Elements (Benchmark Books)
QD181.P1 B43 2001
546'.712—dc21   99-088821 CIP AC

Printed in Hong Kong

Picture credits
Front cover: Jeff Hunter/Image Bank.
Back cover: Hulton Getty.
Albright & Wilson Ltd.: *iii*, 16, 18.
Corbis (UK) Ltd.: George Lepp 23; José Manuel Sanchis Calvete 10; Peter Turnley 11.
Hulton Getty: 12, 21.
Image Bank: Jeff Hunter 15.
Image Select: Ann Ronan Picture Library 7.
Kemira Agro (UK) Ltd.: 20, 22.
Robert Hunt Library: 14.
Robert Opie Collection: 8.
Science Photo Library: Charles D. Winters 6, 30;
Professor K. Seddon & Dr. T. Evans/Queen's University, Belfast 26; National Institutes of Health *i*, 27.
Still Pictures: Mark Edwards 24; Roland Seitre 9.
Tony Stone Images: RNHRD NHS Trust 25.
TRH Pictures: NASA 4.

Series created by Brown Partworks Ltd.
Designed by wda

Contents

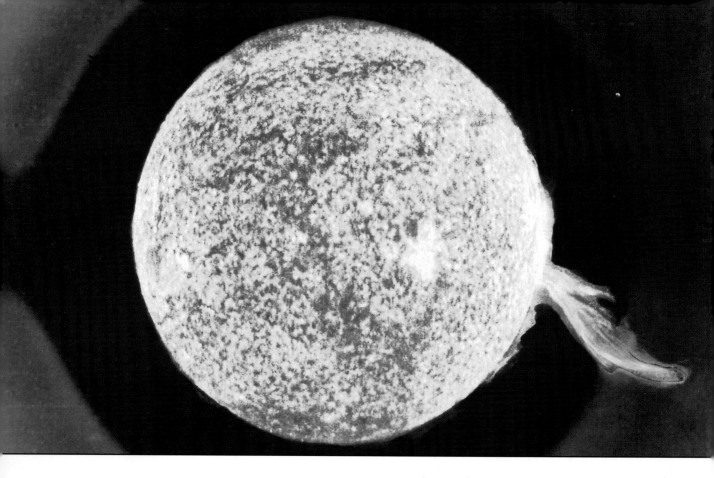

What is phosphorus?

Phosphorus is a nonmetallic chemical element that is essential to all living organisms. The element is not found naturally on Earth but is always combined with other elements, especially oxygen, as compounds. Phosphorus also occurs in the Sun's atmosphere and in meteorites reaching Earth from space. Its main use in industry is in the manufacture of phosphate fertilizers.

The phosphorus atom

Just like all the other chemical elements, phosphorus is made up of tiny particles called atoms. In its nucleus—the tiny but heavy center of an atom—each phosphorus atom has 15 positively charged particles called protons. No other element shares this number, and phosphorus is said to have an "atomic number" of 15.

The nucleus also contains other particles, called neutrons, which are about the same size as protons but uncharged. Some elements have different versions of their atoms, called isotopes, that contain different numbers of neutrons. There is only one natural isotope of phosphorus. It has

15 protons and 16 neutrons, making a total of 31 nuclear particles. Other isotopes can be made artificially but are radioactive, which means they will eventually break up.

Around the nucleus orbit 15 negatively charged electrons. Although electrons are much lighter than protons, they balance the positive electrical charge of the protons, making the atom electrically neutral.

Electrons in atoms occupy orbits called electron shells. Phosphorus has three shells. The first two are filled up and contain two and eight electrons, respectively. The third shell is only partially filled and contains five electrons. The behavior of these outermost electrons determines how phosphorus combines with other atoms to form different chemical compounds.

Forms of phosphorus

Phosphorus is an unusual element, because it exists in several different solid forms called allotropes. The most important allotropes are white phosphorus, red phosphorus, and black phosphorus.

White phosphorus is the main phosphorus allotrope. It is a soft, waxy whitish yellow solid, consisting of four phosphorus atoms joined together as a molecule. White phosphorus is extremely poisonous and bursts into flames if it is exposed to oxygen in the air. For this reason it is normally stored under water.

PHOSPHORUS ATOM

Nucleus | First shell
Second shell
Third shell

Each phosphorus atom contains a nucleus surrounded by three shells of electrons. There are two electrons in the first, or inner, shell, eight electrons in the second shell, and five electrons in the third, or outer, shell. The nucleus contains the neutrons and protons.

DID YOU KNOW?

GLOWING IN THE DARK

The word *phosphorus* comes from the Greek words meaning "light-bringing." The element was given this name because white phosphorus glows in the dark. The glow, which only occurs in the presence of air, is caused by the slow reaction of white phosphorus with oxygen from the air.

PHOSPHORUS FACTS

Chemical symbol	P
Atomic number	15
Relative atomic mass	31
Melting and boiling points	White phosphorus melts at 111°F (44°C) and boils at 536°F (280°C). Red phosphorus sublimes (goes straight from solid to gas) at 780°F (416°C).
Specific gravity	White phosphorus: 1.82. Red phosphorus: 2.34. This means that each form weighs respectively 1.82 and 2.34 times as much as the same volume of water.

Red phosphorus is more stable than white phosphorus and is made up of long chains of phosphorus atoms. A third allotrope, called black phosphorus, can be made under high pressure. This allotrope, however, is not as common as white or red phosphorus.

Using the element

Most phosphorus is used in combination with other elements as compounds, but the element does have some uses. In the past, white phosphorus was used to make matches and as an ingredient in pesticides. Since it is so poisonous, however, its use for these purposes has been stopped. Today, white phosphorus is used to create smokescreens for military operations. Red phosphorus is used in the manufacture of safety matches and fireworks. Phosphorus is also mixed with metallic copper to make a strong alloy called phosphor bronze.

Phosphorus is a highly reactive element and must be stored under water for safe keeping to prevent it from catching fire spontaneously in the air.

The history of phosphorus

Phosphorus was not isolated as an element until late in the 17th century. Its discovery is credited to German chemist Hennig Brand in 1669, although several chemists may have discovered the element independently at the same time. White phosphorus was first prepared by concentrating and distilling human urine.

Phosphorus was a curiosity to early chemists. In the late 18th century, scientists realized that animal bones contained phosphorus and that plants relied on the element to grow properly. Independently, these discoveries led to the growth of the fertilizer industry early in the 19th century.

The popularity of fertilizers required the development of a large-scale industrial process to make elemental phosphorus. Until about 1890, the main method was to separate phosphorus from bone or phosphate rock using sulfuric acid (H_2SO_4) and carbon. In 1888, however, an electric-furnace method was developed by British inventor J. B. Readman. Electric furnaces are still used to make phosphorus today.

The match industry

Another major use for phosphorus in the 19th century was in the matchmaking industry. Before this time, there was no

In the 19th century, phosphorus was manufactured by treating animal bones with concentrated sulfuric acid (H_2SO_4), as shown above. The phosphoric acid (H_3PO_4) produced by this reaction was then heated with carbon to form the element phosphorus.

cheap and convenient way of producing fire at will. In 1831, the first friction matches were introduced. The head of the friction match was primarily made up of white phosphorus but included various

DID YOU KNOW?

OCCUPATIONAL DISEASES

Working with poisonous white phosphorus in match factories severely affected the health of the workers. One of the most serious illnesses they suffered was called "phossy jaw," in which the bones of the jaw decayed. Around the end of the 19th century, use of white phosphorus for matches was banned in most countries.

other chemicals. Striking the head of the match against a surface produced enough heat to ignite the match.

In 1845, Austrian chemist Anton von Schrotter discovered red phosphorus, which is more stable than white phosphorus. For this reason, red phosphorus soon replaced white phosphorus in the matchmaking industry, leading to the development of the first safety match. Instead of being incorporated into the match head, red phosphorus was used to make a strip struck by the match head. The chemical reaction between the strip and other substances in the match head caused the match to ignite. This principle is still used today. "Strike-anywhere" matches are still produced today but use a sulfide of phosphorus instead of the element itself.

This picture shows a box of safety matches dating from the mid 1900s. The strip on the side of the box contains a mixture of red phosphorus and sand.

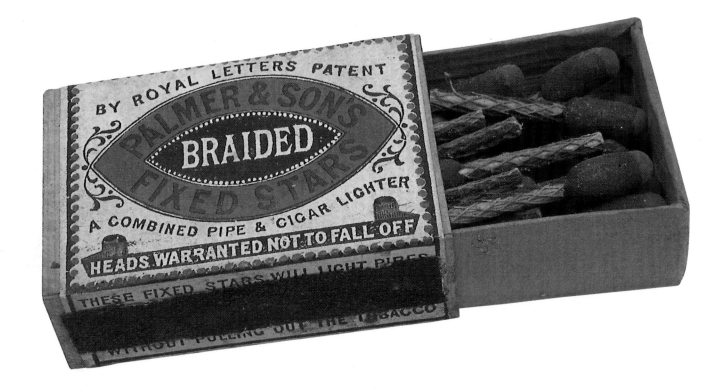

Where phosphorus is found

Workers collect deposits of guano on Guano Island, Peru. Guano is the accumulated waste products of birds and bats and is commonly used as a fertilizer.

Phosphorus is found throughout the universe. It forms part of the atmosphere of the Sun and is also found in meteorites that reach Earth from space. The distribution of phosphorus on Earth has resulted from millions of years of activity under the surface of our planet. Molten material moving upward through the crust, for example, may cool down and separate out into different rocks, some of

them rich in phosphorus. Some of these "igneous" rocks (the word *igneous* means "created by fire") are mined commercially.

Phosphorus forms around 0.1 percent of Earth's crust by weight. It is a highly reactive element and is always found combined with other elements as compounds. Most of the phosphorus on Earth is found in combination with oxygen, and the element nearly always occurs in nature as compounds containing the phosphate ion ($PO_4{}^{3-}$). Phosphorus is essential to most living organisms. As a result, the element is concentrated in living things and their remains. Guano, the accumulated droppings of birds or bats, is rich in phosphorus. Deposits of guano are often collected and used as a fertilizer.

Sedimentary phosphorus

The most important commercial sources of phosphorus are sedimentary rocks. Sedimentary rocks were formed by material laid down on the floors of seas and oceans. Today, the biggest sources are in North Africa. Major deposits are also found in the United States, especially Florida, North Carolina, and southern Idaho.

Geologists (scientists who study the history of Earth and its life) do not completely understand how sedimentary rocks were created. Since phosphate is used by all marine creatures, most of it is continually circulated through the food chain or ends up deep on the ocean floor—too deep to be raised by movements under the surface of Earth.

In some parts of the world, however, phosphate-rich water currents rise from these depths and fertilize shallow coastal waters. This makes possible dense concentrations of offshore marine life. Some of this phosphate is deposited in the shallows as the remains of dead organisms—and possibly washed inshore into bays and estuaries. Later, activity on Earth or sea-level changes are thought to cause some deposits to end up as phosphate rocks on land.

A sample of the mineral apatite ($Ca_5[PO_4]_3F$). In industry, apatite is mined for the phosphorus it contains.

Extraction and purification

This phosphate mine is in the Sahara Desert. North African countries are home to the largest deposits of sedimentary phosphate rocks.

Millions of tons of phosphate-containing rocks are mined each year. Over 90 percent of the total yield is converted to phosphorus compounds, which are used to make fertilizers or for other applications. The remainder is converted to elemental phosphorus.

Mining and processing

Phosphate rocks are fairly easily mined, because they are found near the surface of the soil. Huge digging machines, called draglines, remove overlying material before excavating the phosphate rock. Once collected, the rock is mixed with water and piped to a treatment plant. Here, unwanted materials, called the gangue, are separated out, and the phosphate rock is ground into smaller particles.

The rock is then treated with sulfuric acid (H_2SO_4) or phosphoric acid (H_3PO_4) to dissolve the rock particles. The mix is then ready for processing into fertilizers or other phosphorus compounds; some is converted into elemental phosphorus. This method of treating mined phosphate rock is called the wet process.

Making elemental phosphorus

Compounds such as phosphoric acid are needed in a very pure form for use in certain applications, such as the food industry. Until recently, high-purity phosphoric acid was made only from elemental phosphorus. Today, phosphoric acid produced by the wet process can be purified to the same degree.

Since the late 19th century, the electric furnace has been the main method of isolating pure phosphorus. The furnace is charged with a mixture of phosphate rock, silica (SiO_2), and carbon. A large electric current is then passed through the mixture,

This photograph shows a worker at an electric phosphate smelting furnace in Muscle Shoals, Alabama. The electric-furnace method was developed in the late 19th century and remains the main method of isolating phosphorus from phosphate rock.

heating it to melting point. Unwanted material, called slag, is drained out from the bottom of the furnace, and elemental phosphorus is produced as a gas, along with carbon monoxide (CO) and other gases. The phosphorus gas is condensed using water sprays and collected as white phosphorus. Most furnaces run continuously, making them more efficient.

Chemistry and compounds

Phosphorus is an extremely reactive element. It forms a wide range of different compounds, some of which are very important to industry.

The chemistry of phosphorus

Like most other elements, phosphorus forms bonds with other atoms in two main ways.

In a few compounds, the phosphorus atom accepts electrons from other atoms to become an ion (an electrically charged atom). In the compound sodium phosphide (Na_3P), for example, the phosphorus atom accepts one electron from each sodium atom, becoming a phosphide ion (P^{3-}). This gives phosphorus eight rather than five electrons in its outermost shell, which is a more stable arrangement. By contrast, the sodium atoms become positively charged, so the two elements are held together by electrical attraction. This kind of bond is called an electrovalent, or ionic, bond.

Usually, phosphorus shares its electrons with other atoms, forming what are known as covalent bonds. For example, the bonds between the hydrogen and phosphorus atoms in a phosphine molecule (PH_3) are single covalent bonds made up of two electrons, one from each atom.

ATOMS AT WORK

Phosphorus (III) chloride (PCl_3) is a very important chemical in industry. It is made by passing chlorine gas (Cl_2) over white phosphorus at room temperature.

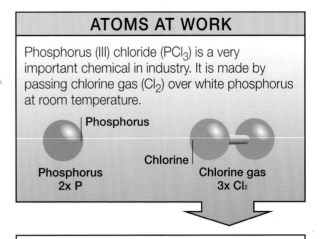

Phosphorus

Chlorine

Phosphorus
2x P

Chlorine gas
3x Cl₂

The heat breaks the bonds holding the chlorine molecules together, and the chlorine atoms are free to form new bonds. A pale green flame can be seen during the reaction.

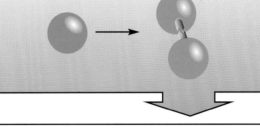

Three chlorine atoms become attached to each phosphorus atom to form phosphorus (III) chloride, which condenses as a colorless liquid.

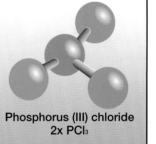

Phosphorus (III) chloride
2x PCl₃

The chemical reaction that takes place can be written like this:

$$2P + 3Cl_2 \rightarrow 2PCl_3$$

The number of atoms of each element is the same on both sides of the equation. The reaction does not stop there, however, because phosphorus (III) chloride will also react with chlorine gas. The substance that forms is called phosphorus (V) chloride (PCl_5).

DID YOU KNOW?

DEALING IN DEATH

The deadly military chemicals called nerve gases, along with many insecticides commonly used by farmers, belong to a group of compounds called organophosphates. These are made by incorporating phosphorus into organic (carbon-containing) chemicals.

Nerve gases and organophosphate insecticides (substances that kill insect pests) are closely connected, both historically and chemically. Nerve gases were developed in Germany in the 1930s. German scientists also developed the first organophosphorus insecticide in 1943. Both these groups of substances work in the same way—they disrupt a substance called cholinesterase that controls the signals sent between nerve cells.

Modern insecticides are much less poisonous to humans than they are to insects. Nevertheless, scientists are still concerned about the long-term effects on natural ecosystems, the health of agricultural workers exposed to them, and the possible danger of insecticide residues in food.

ATOMS AT WORK

Oxygen

Phosphorus

Phosphorus (V) oxide
P_4O_{10}

When red phosphorus burns in air, a compound called phosphorus (V) oxide (P_2O_5) is formed. Phosphorus (V) oxide, often called phosphorus pentoxide, is a white powdery solid. During the reaction, phosphorus pentoxide is produced as a cloud of dense, choking smoke. For this reason, phosphorus pentoxide is often used in military smokescreens.

To make things easy, chemists give phosphorus pentoxide the formula P_2O_5. In fact, each molecule is double this size and has four phosphorus atoms and ten oxygen atoms. The structure is shown above.

Phosphorus is notable, however, because it can share several of its electrons and form a variable number of bonds with other atoms, making the chemistry of the element very complicated. Usually, the

Phosphorus (V) oxide smokescreens are deployed around Simpson Harbor in Rabaul, Papua New Guinea, during a World War II air raid.

A spectacular fireworks display illuminates the night sky. Phosphorus is no longer used to make fireworks. Instead, elements such as barium, copper, sodium, and strontium give the fireworks their bright colors.

equivalent of three or five single bonds are formed. Phosphorus is also strongly attracted to oxygen, which means that molecules consisting of long chains of phosphorus and oxygen atoms can form.

Phosphorus compounds

Phosphoric acid (H_3PO_4) is the most important phosphorus compound (see pages 16 through 19). Other phosphorus compounds are described below.

Phosphorus chlorides. Over 100,000 tons (90,720 tonnes) of phosphorus (III) chloride (PCl_3) are produced each year in the United States. Phosphorus (III) chloride is an important intermediate in the manufacture of organophosphorus compounds. Phosphorus (V) chloride (PCl_5) and phosphorus oxychloride ($POCl_3$) are also used in industry.

Phosphorus oxides. When phosphorus burns in air, the main product is a white powdery solid called phosphorus (V) oxide (P_2O_5). This compound is used to make phosphoric acid by reacting it with water. In a limited air supply, however, phosphorus trioxide (PO_3) is produced instead.

Other phosphorus compounds. Other noteworthy phosphorus compounds include phosphine (PH_3), a highly poisonous gas sometimes used as an insecticide, and phosphorus pentasulfide (P_2S_5), a building block chemical.

Phosphorus acids and salts

The most important compounds of phosphorus in industry are its acids—especially phosphoric (V) acid (H_3PO_4)—and the salts formed from these acids.

Phosphoric acid

Pure phosphoric acid is a colorless crystalline solid with a melting point of 107.6°F (42°C). For industrial use, the acid is usually handled as a concentrated, syrupy solution in water. Impure phosphoric acid is obtained by treating phosphate-containing rocks with sulfuric acid (H_2SO_4). The pure acid is prepared either from the end product of this reaction or by the reaction of phosphorus (V) oxide (P_2O_5) with water. Pure phosphoric acid is a fairly strong acid.

Although the biggest use of phosphoric acid is in the fertilizer industry, it has many other applications. In the metal industry, it is applied to steel to remove rust (iron (III) oxide, Fe_2O_3) and to polish metals such as aluminum. Some specialist cleaning products include phosphoric acid as an ingredient. It is also used in the food and beverage industries—for example, to flavor fizzy cola drinks, where it gives the drink an acid tang. Phosphoric acid is also used to make various phosphate salts.

Purified food-grade phosphoric (V) acid is used to flavor fizzy cola drinks. The compound contributes to the characteristic flavor of the drink.

Phosphate salts

When an acid and an alkali (often called a base) react, a salt and water are the products of the reaction. All salts are composed of positively and negatively

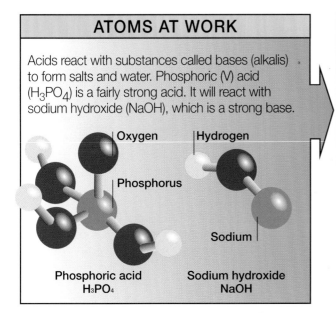

ATOMS AT WORK

Acids react with substances called bases (alkalis) to form salts and water. Phosphoric (V) acid (H_3PO_4) is a fairly strong acid. It will react with sodium hydroxide (NaOH), which is a strong base.

Oxygen

Hydrogen

Phosphorus

Sodium

Phosphoric acid
H_3PO_4

Sodium hydroxide
NaOH

When phosphoric acid is added to sodium hydroxide, the atoms are exchanged. The sodium atom from the sodium hydroxide takes the place of one of the hydrogen atoms from the phosphoric (V) acid.

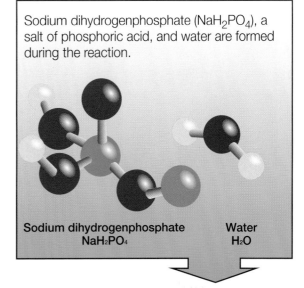

Sodium dihydrogenphosphate (NaH_2PO_4), a salt of phosphoric acid, and water are formed during the reaction.

Sodium dihydrogenphosphate
NaH_2PO_4

Water
H_2O

The chemical reaction that takes place can be written like this:

$$H_3PO_4 + NaOH \rightarrow NaH_2PO_4 + H_2O$$

The number of atoms of each element is the same on both sides of the equation.

The reaction may continue. If two sodium atoms replace the hydrogen atoms, disodium hydrogenphosphate (Na_2HPO_4) forms. If three sodium atoms replace the hydrogen atoms, trisodium phosphate (Na_3PO_4) forms.

charged ions that are bound together by an electrical attraction.

When phosphoric acid combines with a base, such as sodium hydroxide (NaOH), it can form several different salts. This is because the acid may lose one, two, or all three of its hydrogen atoms during the reaction. When all three hydrogens are lost, it becomes a phosphate ion (PO_4^{3-}). The product of the reaction may be sodium dihydrogenphosphate (NaH_2PO_4), disodium hydrogenphosphate (Na_2HPO_4), trisodium phosphate (Na_3PO_4), or a mixture of these. These salts, which are soluble (can dissolve) in water, have many uses, particularly as additives for detergents.

Calcium forms a similar series of phosphate salts. The formulas are different to the sodium salts because the calcium ion has twice the charge of a sodium ion. Most phosphate-containing rocks are a form of

Sodium phosphate salts were once vital ingredients in laundry detergents. Today, many countries have restricted their use due to environmental concerns.

DID YOU KNOW?

DETERGENTS

Phosphate salts, especially those of sodium, were once vital additives for detergents. Known as "builders," these compounds bring several benefits to the detergent. They react with ions in the water to stop them forming a scum with the detergent (a film of impurities on the surface of the water). They also control acidity and stop dirt particles from clumping together. Concerns about pollution have led many U.S. states to pass laws restricting or banning their use.

tricalcium (or just calcium) phosphate $(Ca_3[PO_4]_2)$. To make human-made fertilizers such as superphosphate, calcium phosphate is converted to the more soluble monocalcium phosphate $(Ca[H_2PO_4]_2)$. Calcium phosphates also have uses such as raising agents in the baking industry and supplements for animal feed.

There are also aluminum, ammonium, magnesium, and potassium phosphates, all of which have various uses in industry.

Other phosphorus acids and salts

In addition to phosphoric acid, various other acids of phosphorus exist. Some are created by phosphoric acid molecules joining together in long chains. The simplest of these acids is diphosphoric (V) acid ($H_4P_2O_7$; see the box at right). Their salts are known as polyphosphates. The salt sodium tripolyphosphate (STPP) was once an important additive in detergents.

Two other simple acids of phosphorus have similar and rather confusing names. They are phosphonic and phosphinic acid. Phosphonic acid has the formula H_3PO_3. Also known as phosphorous acid, its salts are called phosphonates or phosphites. Phosphinic acid has the formula H_2PO_2 and is also called hypophosphorous acid.

SEE FOR YOURSELF

DISSOLVING MATERIALS

Most acids, including phosphoric acid, can dissolve or react with some everyday household items. Try leaving items such as coins or cutlery covered with limescale in a cola drink that contains phosphoric acid for a day or two. Can you see what happens? Do the items look cleaner? For comparison, leave the same kinds of objects in orange juice, which contains fruit acids. Does the same thing happen?

PHOSPHATE ACIDS AND SALTS

Phosphorus is an extremely reactive element. It is always found combined with other elements in Earth's crust. It especially forms bonds with oxygen. Four oxygen atoms bond to one phosphorus atom to form the phosphate ion (PO_4^{3-}). Three of the oxygen atoms in a phosphate ion have a negative charge, because the atoms have a free electron in their outer electron shell.

Oxygen

Phosphorus

Phosphate ion
PO_4^{3-}

When three hydrogen atoms bond to the three negatively charged oxygen atoms in a phosphate ion, the compound is called phosphoric (V) acid (H_3PO_4). Phosphoric acid is vital to many industrial processes, including the manufacture of fertilizers and in the food and drink industry.

Hydrogen

Phosphoric acid
H_3PO_4

When phosphoric acid is heated with water, a compound called diphosphoric (V) acid ($H_4P_2O_7$) forms. Diphosphoric (V) acid is an example of a polyphosphate. One oxygen atom joins the two phosphorus atoms from each phosphate group. Other polyphosphates occur with up to ten phosphorus atoms linked by oxygen atoms.

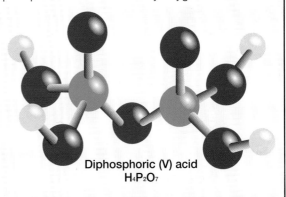

Diphosphoric (V) acid
$H_4P_2O_7$

Fertilizers

Long before phosphorus was discovered as an element, phosphate-rich materials, such as bonemeal (crushed or ground animal bone), were used as fertilizers. In the late 18th century, however, scientists discovered that bones contain phosphorus, and the link between the element and its benefit to plants was established. From the early 1800s, bonemeal and guano (the accumulated excrement of birds and bats) became increasingly used on European farmland.

Superphosphates

The trouble with grinding bones for use as a fertilizer is that the phosphate ions they contain remain largely insoluble, which means the ions are not taken up into a solution. As a result, plants find it difficult to absorb the phosphate ions. A breakthrough came when sulfuric acid (H_2SO_4) was used to dissolve the phosphorus-containing compounds. This was first done commercially by Sir John Bennet Lawes (see the box on page 21). At first, bones were used as the phosphate source. Soon much larger supplies of

These fertilizer granules contain four major plant nutrients: nitrogen, phosphorus, potash alum ($KAl[SO_4]_2.12H_2O$), and phosphate.

phosphate-containing rocks replaced the use of bonemeal. Lawes called the product of the process "superphosphate" (now often called "normal superphosphate"). Normal superphosphate is made up of impure monocalcium phosphate ($CaPO_4$), mixed with gypsum (hydrated calcium sulfate, $CaSO_4.2H_2O$). Simple to produce, normal superphosphate remains popular in many parts of the world, although its use has declined in the United States.

Later, a more concentrated product fertilizer called triple superphosphate was developed. Triple superphosphate is prepared in two stages. First, sulfuric acid is used to break down phosphate rock, resulting in phosphoric acid (H_3PO_4). This is filtered to remove calcium sulfate impurities that form at the same time. The phosphoric acid produced is now applied to more phosphate rock, yielding concentrated monocalcium phosphate.

Sir John Bennet Lawes, shown above, patented the first mineral superphosphate in 1842. His establishment of the first fertilizer factory in the same year laid the foundations for the fertilizer industry.

Other fertilizers

Phosphoric acid can also be used to make other phosphate fertilizers. For example, its reaction with ammonia results in compounds called ammonium phosphates, which are now the most popular phosphate fertilizers in developed countries such as Britain and the United States. Ammonium phosphates provide crops with nitrogen as well as phosphorus. Fertilizers made from phosphoric acid have also been developed for use in specialized agricultural practices. These fertilizers are supplied in solid or liquid form.

Granules of phosphate fertilizer are scattered from a device called a rotary spreader, which is attached to the back of a tractor. Some phosphate fertilizers come as liquids and are sprayed directly onto crops.

Environmental issues

Using phosphorus in the form of phosphate fertilizers has brought great benefits to humankind. Fertilizers have increased agricultural production, reducing famine worldwide. But exploiting the fertilizers has created many environmental problems. Probably the biggest issues relate to mining operations and overfertilization of wild habitats. Scientists are also concerned about the impact of organophosphate insecticides.

Impact of mining

Phosphate mining operations have huge environmental impacts. Strip mining the surface of the ground is the most common method of recovering phosphate deposits.

Strip mining areas of land completely destroys the fragile ecosystems that exist there. Most developed countries have environmental laws that force mining companies to restore the land to its original state, preserving agricultural land or wildlife habitats. Natural ecosystems take a long time to develop, however, and what grows back may not always be the same as what was there before.

Processing phosphate rock also has its drawbacks. Phosphate rock is usually washed to remove unwanted clay particles. These particles are then left to settle in huge "slime ponds." If—as is sometimes the case—the dams around the slime ponds

Phosphorus processing plants such as the one below in Pocatello, Idaho, may be responsible for releasing damaging pollutants into the atmosphere.

burst, clay-rich water can flood the surrounding rivers and lakes and smother all aquatic life.

Eutrophication

Eutrophication is an increase in mineral nutrients in natural water supplies, causing excessive growth of algae (tiny plants) that results in the death of fish. Eutrophication is a natural process, but activities such as agriculture can accelerate the effect.

Phosphates are often the mineral in shortest supply in most habitats and so normally act as a limit on algal growth. The biggest causes of phosphate buildup are runoff from agricultural land and human sewage. Phosphates in detergents are a smaller but significant factor.

The River Po in Italy has been heavily polluted by the discharge of fertilizers and sewage into its waters. Intensive farming practices along the length of the river are thought to be responsible for this pollution.

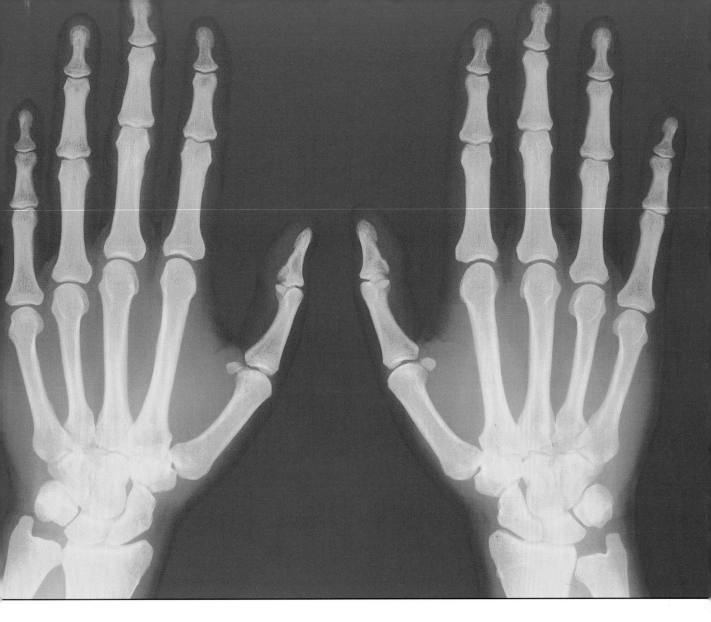

Phosphorus in biology

A color-enhanced X ray shows the bones of the hands. Bone is rich in calcium and phosphorus.

Every living thing, from the simplest bacterium to a human being, is made up of many different kinds of molecules. In the human body, thousands of chemical reactions, collectively called metabolism, are going on all the time to keep each cell alive. Phosphorus—in the form of the phosphate ion (PO_4^{3-})—is very important to this complex chemical activity. Phosphate ions are convenient for the body to handle. Although these ions form stable bonds with other molecules, they can be created or broken easily by enzymes. Enzymes are protein molecules that act as catalysts, promoting and controlling particular chemical reactions.

Phosphorus in cells

When molecules of food enter cells they are broken down in a number of stages. Many of these stages involve adding and removing phosphate ions. This helps the cell to monitor the reactions and obtain the maximum energy from the food molecules. Scientists have learned a great deal about these processes by using a radioactive form of the phosphorus atom called phosphorus-32. In experiments, the presence of radioactive phosphorus atoms in the product of a reaction can easily be detected.

Genes and nucleotides

Deoxyribonucleic acid (DNA), the molecules that encode our genes, contain phosphate groups. These long molecules are built up of individual subunits called nucleotides. Each nucleotide of DNA is made up of three parts—a phosphate ion,

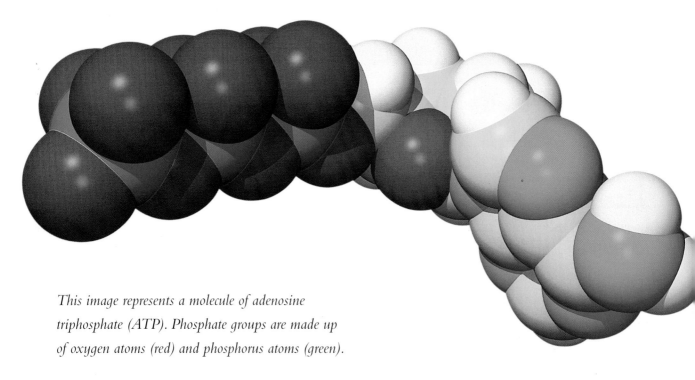

This image represents a molecule of adenosine triphosphate (ATP). Phosphate groups are made up of oxygen atoms (red) and phosphorus atoms (green).

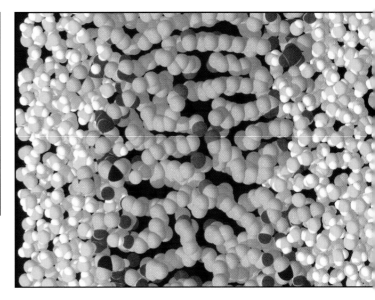

This computer-generated image shows the phospholipid bilayer, which forms the membrane around all living cells. The phosphate-containing "heads" (yellow and white) point outward and the insoluble "tails" (blue) point inward.

a molecule of a sugar called deoxyribose, and one of four nitrogen-containing compounds called bases. In 1953, James Watson (1928–), Francis Crick (1916–), and Rosalind Franklin (1920–1958) showed that DNA was arranged as a "double helix," with two chains of nucleotides that twisted around each other. The sugar and phosphate groups form the "backbone" of the molecule, while the bases, whose arrangement actually codes for the genes, are in the middle. Ribonucleic acid (RNA), a similar molecule to DNA, also contains phosphate groups.

Nucleotides are also very important in their own right. One type, called adenosine triphosphate (ATP), is the main energy-carrying molecule of cells. It is created during the breakdown of foodstuffs and contains a chain of three phosphate groups. When one of these phosphates is removed, energy is released. This is done in a controlled way to help move muscles or

to make other useful molecules, for example. Another nucleotide, called cyclic AMP (adenosine monophosphate), transmits messages within cells.

The bigger picture

Phosphate levels in the body are carefully controlled. Since phosphate occurs in many foods, its deficiency is rare, but some diseases can interfere with its absorption or cause it to leak from the kidneys. In humans, about 85 percent of all phosphate is combined with calcium in bone. This acts as a reservoir for phosphate needed elsewhere. Phosphate is also found in the blood, where it helps to control acidity.

Periodic table

Everything in the universe is made from combinations of substances called elements. Elements are the building blocks of matter. They are made of tiny atoms, which are much too small to see.

The character of an atom depends on how many even tinier particles called protons there are in its center, or nucleus. An element's atomic number is the same as the number of protons.

Scientists have found around 110 different elements. About 90 elements occur naturally on Earth. The rest have been made in experiments.

All these elements are set out on a chart called the periodic table. This lists all the elements in order according to their atomic number.

The elements at the left of the table are metals. Those at the right are nonmetals. Between the metals and the nonmetals are the metalloids, which sometimes act like metals and sometimes like nonmetals.

- On the left of the table are the alkali metals. These elements have just one electron in their outer shells.

- On the right of the periodic table are the noble gases. These elements have full outer shells.

- Elements in the same group have the same number of electrons in their outer shells.

- Elements get more reactive as you go down a group.

- The number of electrons orbiting the nucleus increases down each group.

- The transition metals are in the middle of the table, between Groups II and III.

Group I

Group II

Transition metals

1 H Hydrogen 1

3 Li Lithium 7	4 Be Beryllium 9

11 Na Sodium 23	12 Mg Magnesium 24

19 K Potassium 39	20 Ca Calcium 40	21 Sc Scandium 45	22 Ti Titanium 48	23 V Vanadium 51	24 Cr Chromium 52	25 Mn Manganese 55	26 Fe Iron 56	27 Co Cobalt 59
37 Rb Rubidium 85	38 Sr Strontium 88	39 Y Yttrium 89	40 Zr Zirconium 91	41 Nb Niobium 93	42 Mo Molybdenum 96	43 Tc Technetium (98)	44 Ru Ruthenium 101	45 Rh Rhodium 103
55 Cs Cesium 133	56 Ba Barium 137	71 Lu Lutetium 175	72 Hf Hafnium 179	73 Ta Tantalum 181	74 W Tungsten 184	75 Re Rhenium 186	76 Os Osmium 190	77 Ir Iridium 192
87 Fr Francium 223	88 Ra Radium 226	103 Lr Lawrencium (260)	104 Unq Unnilquadium (261)	105 Unp Unnilpentium (262)	106 Unh Unnilhexium (263)	107 Uns Unnilseptium (?)	108 Uno Unniloctium (?)	109 Une Unnilenium (?)

Lanthanide elements

Actinide elements

57 La Lanthanum 39	58 Ce Cerium 140	59 Pr Praseodymium 141	60 Nd Neodymium 144	61 Pm Promethium (145)
89 Ac Actinium 227	90 Th Thorium 232	91 Pa Protactinium 231	92 U Uranium 238	93 Np Neptunium (237)

The horizontal rows are called periods. As you go across a period, the atomic number increases by one from each element to the next. The vertical columns are called groups. Elements get heavier as you go down a group. All the elements in a group have the same number of electrons in their outer shells. This means they react in similar ways.

The transition metals fall between Groups II and III. Their electron shells fill up in an unusual way. The lanthanide elements and the actinide elements are set apart from the main table to make it easier to read. All the lanthanide elements and the actinide elements are quite rare.

Phosphorus in the table

Phosphorus has atomic number 15, which tells us that it has 15 protons in its nucleus. It is positioned on the right-hand side of the periodic table among the nonmetals.

Along with nitrogen, arsenic, antimony, and bismuth, phosphorus forms Group V of the periodic table. Each Group V element has five electrons in its outer shell.

Metals
Metalloids (semimetals)
Nonmetals

			Group III	Group IV	Group V	Group VI	Group VII	Group VIII
								2 He Helium 4
			5 B Boron 11	6 C Carbon 12	7 N Nitrogen 14	8 O Oxygen 16	9 F Fluorine 19	10 Ne Neon 20
			13 Al Aluminum 27	14 Si Silicon 28	15 P Phosphorus 31	16 S Phosphorus 32	17 Cl Chlorine 35	18 Ar Argon 40
28 Ni Nickel 59	29 Cu Copper 64	30 Zn Zinc 65	31 Ga Gallium 70	32 Ge Germanium 73	33 As Arsenic 75	34 Se Selenium 79	35 Br Bromine 80	36 Kr Krypton 84
46 Pd Palladium 106	47 Ag Silver 108	48 Cd Cadmium 112	49 In Indium 115	50 Sn Tin 119	51 Sb Antimony 122	52 Te Tellurium 128	53 I Iodine 127	54 Xe Xenon 131
78 Pt Platinum 195	79 Au Gold 197	80 Hg Mercury 201	81 Tl Thallium 204	82 Pb Lead 207	83 Bi Bismuth 209	84 Po Polonium (209)	85 At Astatine (210)	86 Rn Radon (222)

Key:
15
P
Phosphorus
31
Atomic (proton) number
Symbol
Name
Atomic mass

62 Sm Samarium 150	63 Eu Europium 152	64 Gd Gadolinium 157	65 Tb Terbium 159	66 Dy Dysprosium 163	67 Ho Holmium 165	68 Er Erbium 167	69 Tm Thulium 169	70 Yb Ytterbium 173
94 Pu Plutonium (244)	95 Am Americium (243)	96 Cm Curium (247)	97 Bk Berkelium (247)	98 Cf Californium (251)	99 Es Einsteinium (252)	100 Fm Fermium (257)	101 Md Mendelevium (258)	102 No Nobelium (259)

Chemical reactions

Chemical reactions are going on all the time. Some reactions involve just two substances; others many more. But whenever a reaction takes place, at least one substance is changed.

In a chemical reaction, the atoms stay the same. But they join up in different combinations to form new molecules.

Writing an equation

Equations are a quick and easy way of showing what happens in a chemical reaction. They show the number of atoms

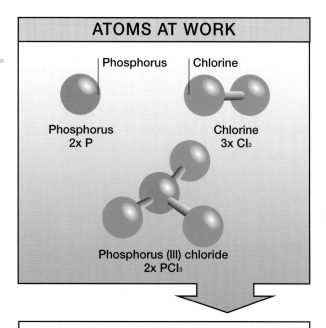

ATOMS AT WORK

Phosphorus

Chlorine

Phosphorus
2x P

Chlorine
3x Cl$_2$

Phosphorus (III) chloride
2x PCl$_3$

The chemical reaction that takes place when phosphorus reacts with chlorine looks like this:

$$2P + 3Cl_2 \rightarrow 2PCl_3$$

The number of phosphorus atoms and chlorine atoms is the same on both sides of the equation.

and molecules at the beginning and the end of a chemical reaction.

When the numbers of each atom on both sides of the equation are equal, the equation is balanced. If the numbers are not equal, something must be wrong. So the chemist looks at the equation again and adjusts the number of atoms involved until the equation balances.

This picture shows the violent reaction that occurs when chlorine gas reacts with white phosphorus. Phosphorus and chlorine atoms combine to form phosphorus (III) chloride. In an excess of chlorine gas, chlorine atoms will combine with phosphorus (III) chloride to form phosphorus (V) chloride.

Glossary

allotrope: A different form of the same element in which the atoms are arranged in a different pattern.

atom: The smallest part of an element that has all the properties of that element. Each atom is less than a millionth of an inch in diameter.

atomic mass: The number of protons and neutrons in an atom.

atomic number: The number of protons in an atom.

bond: The attraction between two atoms that holds them together.

catalyst: Something that makes a chemical reaction happen more quickly.

compound: A substance made of two or more elements that have combined together chemically.

electron: A tiny particle with a negative charge. Electrons are found inside atoms, where they move around the nucleus in layers called electron shells.

eutrophication: An increase in mineral nutrients in natural water supplies, causing excessive growth of algae.

igneous rock: A rock that develops from volcanic lava on Earth's surface or magma deep underground.

isotopes: Atoms of an element with the same number of protons and neutrons but different numbers of neutrons.

gangue: The worthless material in which valuable metals or minerals occur.

guano: The accumulated droppings of birds or bats.

metal: An element on the left-hand side of the periodic table.

neutron: A tiny particle with no electrical charge. It is found in the nucleus of every atom.

nonmetal: An element on the right-hand side of the periodic table.

nucleus: The center of an atom. It contains protons and neutrons.

ore: A collection of minerals from which a desired element is usually extracted.

periodic table: A chart of all the chemical elements laid out in order of their atomic number.

products: The substances formed in a chemical reaction.

proton: A tiny particle with a positive charge. Protons are found inside the nucleus of an atom.

reactants: The substances that react together in a chemical reaction.

scum: A film of impurities that forms on the surface of water when detergents react with ions in the water.

sedimentary rock: Rock formed by the accumulation of particles derived from preexisting rocks.

sublimation: Conversion of a solid directly into a gas without passing through the liquid phase.

Index

ML